Date	For	Name of Caller & Company	Time of Call	Delivery Time
Phone Number:		**Email:**		☐ Urgent
Message:				☐ Returned Call
				☐ Stopped By
				☐ Please Call
				☐ Wants to See You

Date	For	Name of Caller & Company	Time of Call	Delivery Time
Phone Number:		**Email:**		☐ Urgent
Message:				☐ Returned Call
				☐ Stopped By
				☐ Please Call
				☐ Wants to See You

Date	For	Name of Caller & Company	Time of Call	Delivery Time
Phone Number:		**Email:**		☐ Urgent
Message:				☐ Returned Call
				☐ Stopped By
				☐ Please Call
				☐ Wants to See You

Date	For	Name of Caller & Company	Time of Call	Delivery Time
Phone Number:	**Email:**			☐ Urgent
Message:				☐ Returned Call
				☐ Stopped By
				☐ Please Call
				☐ Wants to See You

Date	For	Name of Caller & Company	Time of Call	Delivery Time
Phone Number:	**Email:**			☐ Urgent
Message:				☐ Returned Call
				☐ Stopped By
				☐ Please Call
				☐ Wants to See You

Date	For	Name of Caller & Company	Time of Call	Delivery Time
Phone Number:	**Email:**			☐ Urgent
Message:				☐ Returned Call
				☐ Stopped By
				☐ Please Call
				☐ Wants to See You

Date	For	Name of Caller & Company	Time of Call	Delivery Time
Phone Number:		Email:		☐ Urgent
Message:				☐ Returned Call
				☐ Stopped By
				☐ Please Call
				☐ Wants to See You

Date	For	Name of Caller & Company	Time of Call	Delivery Time
Phone Number:		Email:		☐ Urgent
Message:				☐ Returned Call
				☐ Stopped By
				☐ Please Call
				☐ Wants to See You

Date	For	Name of Caller & Company	Time of Call	Delivery Time
Phone Number:		Email:		☐ Urgent
Message:				☐ Returned Call
				☐ Stopped By
				☐ Please Call
				☐ Wants to See You

Date	For	Name of Caller & Company	Time of Call	Delivery Time

Phone Number:	Email:	☐ Urgent
Message:		☐ Returned Call
		☐ Stopped By
		☐ Please Call
		☐ Wants to See You

Date	For	Name of Caller & Company	Time of Call	Delivery Time

Phone Number:	Email:	☐ Urgent
Message:		☐ Returned Call
		☐ Stopped By
		☐ Please Call
		☐ Wants to See You

Date	For	Name of Caller & Company	Time of Call	Delivery Time

Phone Number:	Email:	☐ Urgent
Message:		☐ Returned Call
		☐ Stopped By
		☐ Please Call
		☐ Wants to See You

Date	For	Name of Caller & Company	Time of Call	Delivery Time

Phone Number:	Email:	☐ Urgent
Message:		☐ Returned Call
		☐ Stopped By
		☐ Please Call
		☐ Wants to See You

Date	For	Name of Caller & Company	Time of Call	Delivery Time

Phone Number:	Email:	☐ Urgent
Message:		☐ Returned Call
		☐ Stopped By
		☐ Please Call
		☐ Wants to See You

Date	For	Name of Caller & Company	Time of Call	Delivery Time

Phone Number:	Email:	☐ Urgent
Message:		☐ Returned Call
		☐ Stopped By
		☐ Please Call
		☐ Wants to See You

Date	For	Name of Caller & Company	Time of Call	Delivery Time

Phone Number:	Email:	☐ Urgent
Message:		☐ Returned Call
		☐ Stopped By
		☐ Please Call
		☐ Wants to See You

Date	For	Name of Caller & Company	Time of Call	Delivery Time

Phone Number:	Email:	☐ Urgent
Message:		☐ Returned Call
		☐ Stopped By
		☐ Please Call
		☐ Wants to See You

Date	For	Name of Caller & Company	Time of Call	Delivery Time

Phone Number:	Email:	☐ Urgent
Message:		☐ Returned Call
		☐ Stopped By
		☐ Please Call
		☐ Wants to See You

Date	For	Name of Caller & Company	Time of Call	Delivery Time

Phone Number:	Email:	☐ Urgent
Message:		☐ Returned Call
		☐ Stopped By
		☐ Please Call
		☐ Wants to See You

Date	For	Name of Caller & Company	Time of Call	Delivery Time

Phone Number:	Email:	☐ Urgent
Message:		☐ Returned Call
		☐ Stopped By
		☐ Please Call
		☐ Wants to See You

Date	For	Name of Caller & Company	Time of Call	Delivery Time

Phone Number:	Email:	☐ Urgent
Message:		☐ Returned Call
		☐ Stopped By
		☐ Please Call
		☐ Wants to See You

Date	For	Name of Caller & Company	Time of Call	Delivery Time

Phone Number:	Email:	☐ Urgent
Message:		☐ Returned Call
		☐ Stopped By
		☐ Please Call
		☐ Wants to See You

Date	For	Name of Caller & Company	Time of Call	Delivery Time

Phone Number:	Email:	☐ Urgent
Message:		☐ Returned Call
		☐ Stopped By
		☐ Please Call
		☐ Wants to See You

Date	For	Name of Caller & Company	Time of Call	Delivery Time

Phone Number:	Email:	☐ Urgent
Message:		☐ Returned Call
		☐ Stopped By
		☐ Please Call
		☐ Wants to See You

Date	For	Name of Caller & Company	Time of Call	Delivery Time

Phone Number:	Email:	☐ Urgent
Message:		☐ Returned Call
		☐ Stopped By
		☐ Please Call
		☐ Wants to See You

Date	For	Name of Caller & Company	Time of Call	Delivery Time

Phone Number:	Email:	☐ Urgent
Message:		☐ Returned Call
		☐ Stopped By
		☐ Please Call
		☐ Wants to See You

Date	For	Name of Caller & Company	Time of Call	Delivery Time

Phone Number:	Email:	☐ Urgent
Message:		☐ Returned Call
		☐ Stopped By
		☐ Please Call
		☐ Wants to See You

Date	For	Name of Caller & Company	Time of Call	Delivery Time

Phone Number:	Email:	☐ Urgent
Message:		☐ Returned Call
		☐ Stopped By
		☐ Please Call
		☐ Wants to See You

Date	For	Name of Caller & Company	Time of Call	Delivery Time

Phone Number:	Email:	☐ Urgent
Message:		☐ Returned Call
		☐ Stopped By
		☐ Please Call
		☐ Wants to See You

Date	For	Name of Caller & Company	Time of Call	Delivery Time

Phone Number:	Email:	☐ Urgent
Message:		☐ Returned Call
		☐ Stopped By
		☐ Please Call
		☐ Wants to See You

Date	For	Name of Caller & Company	Time of Call	Delivery Time

Phone Number:	Email:	☐ Urgent
Message:		☐ Returned Call
		☐ Stopped By
		☐ Please Call
		☐ Wants to See You

Date	For	Name of Caller & Company	Time of Call	Delivery Time

Phone Number:	Email:	☐ Urgent
Message:		☐ Returned Call
		☐ Stopped By
		☐ Please Call
		☐ Wants to See You

Date	For	Name of Caller & Company	Time of Call	Delivery Time

Phone Number:	Email:	☐ Urgent
Message:		☐ Returned Call
		☐ Stopped By
		☐ Please Call
		☐ Wants to See You

Date	For	Name of Caller & Company	Time of Call	Delivery Time

Phone Number:	Email:	☐ Urgent
Message:		☐ Returned Call
		☐ Stopped By
		☐ Please Call
		☐ Wants to See You

Date	For	Name of Caller & Company	Time of Call	Delivery Time

Phone Number:	Email:	☐ Urgent
Message:		☐ Returned Call
		☐ Stopped By
		☐ Please Call
		☐ Wants to See You

Date	For	Name of Caller & Company	Time of Call	Delivery Time

Phone Number:	Email:	☐ Urgent
Message:		☐ Returned Call
		☐ Stopped By
		☐ Please Call
		☐ Wants to See You

Date	For	Name of Caller & Company	Time of Call	Delivery Time
Phone Number:		Email:		☐ Urgent
Message:				☐ Returned Call
				☐ Stopped By
				☐ Please Call
				☐ Wants to See You

Date	For	Name of Caller & Company	Time of Call	Delivery Time
Phone Number:		Email:		☐ Urgent
Message:				☐ Returned Call
				☐ Stopped By
				☐ Please Call
				☐ Wants to See You

Date	For	Name of Caller & Company	Time of Call	Delivery Time
Phone Number:		Email:		☐ Urgent
Message:				☐ Returned Call
				☐ Stopped By
				☐ Please Call
				☐ Wants to See You

Date	For	Name of Caller & Company	Time of Call	Delivery Time
Phone Number:		Email:		☐ Urgent
Message:				☐ Returned Call
				☐ Stopped By
				☐ Please Call
				☐ Wants to See You

Date	For	Name of Caller & Company	Time of Call	Delivery Time
Phone Number:		Email:		☐ Urgent
Message:				☐ Returned Call
				☐ Stopped By
				☐ Please Call
				☐ Wants to See You

Date	For	Name of Caller & Company	Time of Call	Delivery Time
Phone Number:		Email:		☐ Urgent
Message:				☐ Returned Call
				☐ Stopped By
				☐ Please Call
				☐ Wants to See You

Date	For	Name of Caller & Company	Time of Call	Delivery Time
Phone Number:	Email:			☐ Urgent
Message:				☐ Returned Call
				☐ Stopped By
				☐ Please Call
				☐ Wants to See You

Date	For	Name of Caller & Company	Time of Call	Delivery Time
Phone Number:	Email:			☐ Urgent
Message:				☐ Returned Call
				☐ Stopped By
				☐ Please Call
				☐ Wants to See You

Date	For	Name of Caller & Company	Time of Call	Delivery Time
Phone Number:	Email:			☐ Urgent
Message:				☐ Returned Call
				☐ Stopped By
				☐ Please Call
				☐ Wants to See You

Date	For	Name of Caller & Company	Time of Call	Delivery Time
Phone Number:	Email:			☐ Urgent
Message:				☐ Returned Call
				☐ Stopped By
				☐ Please Call
				☐ Wants to See You

Date	For	Name of Caller & Company	Time of Call	Delivery Time
Phone Number:	Email:			☐ Urgent
Message:				☐ Returned Call
				☐ Stopped By
				☐ Please Call
				☐ Wants to See You

Date	For	Name of Caller & Company	Time of Call	Delivery Time
Phone Number:	Email:			☐ Urgent
Message:				☐ Returned Call
				☐ Stopped By
				☐ Please Call
				☐ Wants to See You

Date	For	Name of Caller & Company	Time of Call	Delivery Time

Phone Number:	Email:	☐ Urgent
Message:		☐ Returned Call
		☐ Stopped By
		☐ Please Call
		☐ Wants to See You

Date	For	Name of Caller & Company	Time of Call	Delivery Time

Phone Number:	Email:	☐ Urgent
Message:		☐ Returned Call
		☐ Stopped By
		☐ Please Call
		☐ Wants to See You

Date	For	Name of Caller & Company	Time of Call	Delivery Time

Phone Number:	Email:	☐ Urgent
Message:		☐ Returned Call
		☐ Stopped By
		☐ Please Call
		☐ Wants to See You

Date	For	Name of Caller & Company	Time of Call	Delivery Time

Phone Number:	Email:	☐ Urgent
Message:		☐ Returned Call
		☐ Stopped By
		☐ Please Call
		☐ Wants to See You

Date	For	Name of Caller & Company	Time of Call	Delivery Time

Phone Number:	Email:	☐ Urgent
Message:		☐ Returned Call
		☐ Stopped By
		☐ Please Call
		☐ Wants to See You

Date	For	Name of Caller & Company	Time of Call	Delivery Time

Phone Number:	Email:	☐ Urgent
Message:		☐ Returned Call
		☐ Stopped By
		☐ Please Call
		☐ Wants to See You

Date	For	Name of Caller & Company	Time of Call	Delivery Time

Phone Number:	Email:	☐ Urgent
Message:		☐ Returned Call
		☐ Stopped By
		☐ Please Call
		☐ Wants to See You

Date	For	Name of Caller & Company	Time of Call	Delivery Time

Phone Number:	Email:	☐ Urgent
Message:		☐ Returned Call
		☐ Stopped By
		☐ Please Call
		☐ Wants to See You

Date	For	Name of Caller & Company	Time of Call	Delivery Time

Phone Number:	Email:	☐ Urgent
Message:		☐ Returned Call
		☐ Stopped By
		☐ Please Call
		☐ Wants to See You

Date	For	Name of Caller & Company	Time of Call	Delivery Time

Phone Number:		Email:		☐ Urgent
Message:				☐ Returned Call
				☐ Stopped By
				☐ Please Call
				☐ Wants to See You

Date	For	Name of Caller & Company	Time of Call	Delivery Time

Phone Number:		Email:		☐ Urgent
Message:				☐ Returned Call
				☐ Stopped By
				☐ Please Call
				☐ Wants to See You

Date	For	Name of Caller & Company	Time of Call	Delivery Time

Phone Number:		Email:		☐ Urgent
Message:				☐ Returned Call
				☐ Stopped By
				☐ Please Call
				☐ Wants to See You

Date	For	Name of Caller & Company	Time of Call	Delivery Time

Phone Number:	Email:	☐ Urgent
Message:		☐ Returned Call
		☐ Stopped By
		☐ Please Call
		☐ Wants to See You

Date	For	Name of Caller & Company	Time of Call	Delivery Time

Phone Number:	Email:	☐ Urgent
Message:		☐ Returned Call
		☐ Stopped By
		☐ Please Call
		☐ Wants to See You

Date	For	Name of Caller & Company	Time of Call	Delivery Time

Phone Number:	Email:	☐ Urgent
Message:		☐ Returned Call
		☐ Stopped By
		☐ Please Call
		☐ Wants to See You

Date	For	Name of Caller & Company	Time of Call	Delivery Time

Phone Number:	**Email:**	☐ Urgent
Message:		☐ Returned Call
		☐ Stopped By
		☐ Please Call
		☐ Wants to See You

Date	For	Name of Caller & Company	Time of Call	Delivery Time

Phone Number:	**Email:**	☐ Urgent
Message:		☐ Returned Call
		☐ Stopped By
		☐ Please Call
		☐ Wants to See You

Date	For	Name of Caller & Company	Time of Call	Delivery Time

Phone Number:	**Email:**	☐ Urgent
Message:		☐ Returned Call
		☐ Stopped By
		☐ Please Call
		☐ Wants to See You

Date	For	Name of Caller & Company	Time of Call	Delivery Time

Phone Number:	Email:	☐ Urgent
Message:		☐ Returned Call
		☐ Stopped By
		☐ Please Call
		☐ Wants to See You

Date	For	Name of Caller & Company	Time of Call	Delivery Time

Phone Number:	Email:	☐ Urgent
Message:		☐ Returned Call
		☐ Stopped By
		☐ Please Call
		☐ Wants to See You

Date	For	Name of Caller & Company	Time of Call	Delivery Time

Phone Number:	Email:	☐ Urgent
Message:		☐ Returned Call
		☐ Stopped By
		☐ Please Call
		☐ Wants to See You

Date	For	Name of Caller & Company	Time of Call	Delivery Time
Phone Number:		Email:		☐ Urgent
Message:				☐ Returned Call
				☐ Stopped By
				☐ Please Call
				☐ Wants to See You

Date	For	Name of Caller & Company	Time of Call	Delivery Time
Phone Number:		Email:		☐ Urgent
Message:				☐ Returned Call
				☐ Stopped By
				☐ Please Call
				☐ Wants to See You

Date	For	Name of Caller & Company	Time of Call	Delivery Time
Phone Number:		Email:		☐ Urgent
Message:				☐ Returned Call
				☐ Stopped By
				☐ Please Call
				☐ Wants to See You

Date	For	Name of Caller & Company	Time of Call	Delivery Time

Phone Number:	Email:	
Message:		☐ Urgent
		☐ Returned Call
		☐ Stopped By
		☐ Please Call
		☐ Wants to See You

Date	For	Name of Caller & Company	Time of Call	Delivery Time

Phone Number:	Email:	
Message:		☐ Urgent
		☐ Returned Call
		☐ Stopped By
		☐ Please Call
		☐ Wants to See You

Date	For	Name of Caller & Company	Time of Call	Delivery Time

Phone Number:	Email:	
Message:		☐ Urgent
		☐ Returned Call
		☐ Stopped By
		☐ Please Call
		☐ Wants to See You

Date	For	Name of Caller & Company	Time of Call	Delivery Time
Phone Number:	Email:			☐ Urgent
Message:				☐ Returned Call
				☐ Stopped By
				☐ Please Call
				☐ Wants to See You

Date	For	Name of Caller & Company	Time of Call	Delivery Time
Phone Number:	Email:			☐ Urgent
Message:				☐ Returned Call
				☐ Stopped By
				☐ Please Call
				☐ Wants to See You

Date	For	Name of Caller & Company	Time of Call	Delivery Time
Phone Number:	Email:			☐ Urgent
Message:				☐ Returned Call
				☐ Stopped By
				☐ Please Call
				☐ Wants to See You

Date	For	Name of Caller & Company	Time of Call	Delivery Time

Phone Number:	Email:	☐ Urgent
Message:		☐ Returned Call
		☐ Stopped By
		☐ Please Call
		☐ Wants to See You

Date	For	Name of Caller & Company	Time of Call	Delivery Time

Phone Number:	Email:	☐ Urgent
Message:		☐ Returned Call
		☐ Stopped By
		☐ Please Call
		☐ Wants to See You

Date	For	Name of Caller & Company	Time of Call	Delivery Time

Phone Number:	Email:	☐ Urgent
Message:		☐ Returned Call
		☐ Stopped By
		☐ Please Call
		☐ Wants to See You

Date	For	Name of Caller & Company	Time of Call	Delivery Time

Phone Number:	Email:	☐ Urgent
Message:		☐ Returned Call
		☐ Stopped By
		☐ Please Call
		☐ Wants to See You

Date	For	Name of Caller & Company	Time of Call	Delivery Time

Phone Number:	Email:	☐ Urgent
Message:		☐ Returned Call
		☐ Stopped By
		☐ Please Call
		☐ Wants to See You

Date	For	Name of Caller & Company	Time of Call	Delivery Time

Phone Number:	Email:	☐ Urgent
Message:		☐ Returned Call
		☐ Stopped By
		☐ Please Call
		☐ Wants to See You

Date	For	Name of Caller & Company	Time of Call	Delivery Time

Phone Number:	Email:	☐ Urgent
Message:		☐ Returned Call
		☐ Stopped By
		☐ Please Call
		☐ Wants to See You

Date	For	Name of Caller & Company	Time of Call	Delivery Time

Phone Number:	Email:	☐ Urgent
Message:		☐ Returned Call
		☐ Stopped By
		☐ Please Call
		☐ Wants to See You

Date	For	Name of Caller & Company	Time of Call	Delivery Time

Phone Number:	Email:	☐ Urgent
Message:		☐ Returned Call
		☐ Stopped By
		☐ Please Call
		☐ Wants to See You

Date	For	Name of Caller & Company	Time of Call	Delivery Time

Phone Number:	Email:	☐ Urgent
Message:		☐ Returned Call
		☐ Stopped By
		☐ Please Call
		☐ Wants to See You

Date	For	Name of Caller & Company	Time of Call	Delivery Time

Phone Number:	Email:	☐ Urgent
Message:		☐ Returned Call
		☐ Stopped By
		☐ Please Call
		☐ Wants to See You

Date	For	Name of Caller & Company	Time of Call	Delivery Time

Phone Number:	Email:	☐ Urgent
Message:		☐ Returned Call
		☐ Stopped By
		☐ Please Call
		☐ Wants to See You

Date	For	Name of Caller & Company	Time of Call	Delivery Time

Phone Number:	Email:	☐ Urgent
Message:		☐ Returned Call
		☐ Stopped By
		☐ Please Call
		☐ Wants to See You

Date	For	Name of Caller & Company	Time of Call	Delivery Time

Phone Number:	Email:	☐ Urgent
Message:		☐ Returned Call
		☐ Stopped By
		☐ Please Call
		☐ Wants to See You

Date	For	Name of Caller & Company	Time of Call	Delivery Time

Phone Number:	Email:	☐ Urgent
Message:		☐ Returned Call
		☐ Stopped By
		☐ Please Call
		☐ Wants to See You

Date	For	Name of Caller & Company	Time of Call	Delivery Time

Phone Number:	Email:	☐ Urgent
Message:		☐ Returned Call
		☐ Stopped By
		☐ Please Call
		☐ Wants to See You

Date	For	Name of Caller & Company	Time of Call	Delivery Time

Phone Number:	Email:	☐ Urgent
Message:		☐ Returned Call
		☐ Stopped By
		☐ Please Call
		☐ Wants to See You

Date	For	Name of Caller & Company	Time of Call	Delivery Time

Phone Number:	Email:	☐ Urgent
Message:		☐ Returned Call
		☐ Stopped By
		☐ Please Call
		☐ Wants to See You

Date	For	Name of Caller & Company	Time of Call	Delivery Time
Phone Number:		Email:		☐ Urgent
Message:				☐ Returned Call
				☐ Stopped By
				☐ Please Call
				☐ Wants to See You

Date	For	Name of Caller & Company	Time of Call	Delivery Time
Phone Number:		Email:		☐ Urgent
Message:				☐ Returned Call
				☐ Stopped By
				☐ Please Call
				☐ Wants to See You

Date	For	Name of Caller & Company	Time of Call	Delivery Time
Phone Number:		Email:		☐ Urgent
Message:				☐ Returned Call
				☐ Stopped By
				☐ Please Call
				☐ Wants to See You

Date	For	Name of Caller & Company	Time of Call	Delivery Time
Phone Number:	Email:			☐ Urgent
Message:				☐ Returned Call
				☐ Stopped By
				☐ Please Call
				☐ Wants to See You

Date	For	Name of Caller & Company	Time of Call	Delivery Time
Phone Number:	Email:			☐ Urgent
Message:				☐ Returned Call
				☐ Stopped By
				☐ Please Call
				☐ Wants to See You

Date	For	Name of Caller & Company	Time of Call	Delivery Time
Phone Number:	Email:			☐ Urgent
Message:				☐ Returned Call
				☐ Stopped By
				☐ Please Call
				☐ Wants to See You

Date	For	Name of Caller & Company	Time of Call	Delivery Time

Phone Number:	Email:	☐ Urgent
Message:		☐ Returned Call
		☐ Stopped By
		☐ Please Call
		☐ Wants to See You

Date	For	Name of Caller & Company	Time of Call	Delivery Time

Phone Number:	Email:	☐ Urgent
Message:		☐ Returned Call
		☐ Stopped By
		☐ Please Call
		☐ Wants to See You

Date	For	Name of Caller & Company	Time of Call	Delivery Time

Phone Number:	Email:	☐ Urgent
Message:		☐ Returned Call
		☐ Stopped By
		☐ Please Call
		☐ Wants to See You

Date	For	Name of Caller & Company	Time of Call	Delivery Time

Phone Number:	Email:	☐ Urgent
Message:		☐ Returned Call
		☐ Stopped By
		☐ Please Call
		☐ Wants to See You

Date	For	Name of Caller & Company	Time of Call	Delivery Time

Phone Number:	Email:	☐ Urgent
Message:		☐ Returned Call
		☐ Stopped By
		☐ Please Call
		☐ Wants to See You

Date	For	Name of Caller & Company	Time of Call	Delivery Time

Phone Number:	Email:	☐ Urgent
Message:		☐ Returned Call
		☐ Stopped By
		☐ Please Call
		☐ Wants to See You

Date	For	Name of Caller & Company	Time of Call	Delivery Time

Phone Number:	Email:	☐ Urgent
Message:		☐ Returned Call
		☐ Stopped By
		☐ Please Call
		☐ Wants to See You

Date	For	Name of Caller & Company	Time of Call	Delivery Time

Phone Number:	Email:	☐ Urgent
Message:		☐ Returned Call
		☐ Stopped By
		☐ Please Call
		☐ Wants to See You

Date	For	Name of Caller & Company	Time of Call	Delivery Time

Phone Number:	Email:	☐ Urgent
Message:		☐ Returned Call
		☐ Stopped By
		☐ Please Call
		☐ Wants to See You

Date	For	Name of Caller & Company	Time of Call	Delivery Time

Phone Number:	Email:	☐ Urgent
Message:		☐ Returned Call
		☐ Stopped By
		☐ Please Call
		☐ Wants to See You

Date	For	Name of Caller & Company	Time of Call	Delivery Time

Phone Number:	Email:	☐ Urgent
Message:		☐ Returned Call
		☐ Stopped By
		☐ Please Call
		☐ Wants to See You

Date	For	Name of Caller & Company	Time of Call	Delivery Time

Phone Number:	Email:	☐ Urgent
Message:		☐ Returned Call
		☐ Stopped By
		☐ Please Call
		☐ Wants to See You

Date	For	Name of Caller & Company	Time of Call	Delivery Time
Phone Number:	Email:			☐ Urgent
Message:				☐ Returned Call
				☐ Stopped By
				☐ Please Call
				☐ Wants to See You

Date	For	Name of Caller & Company	Time of Call	Delivery Time
Phone Number:	Email:			☐ Urgent
Message:				☐ Returned Call
				☐ Stopped By
				☐ Please Call
				☐ Wants to See You

Date	For	Name of Caller & Company	Time of Call	Delivery Time
Phone Number:	Email:			☐ Urgent
Message:				☐ Returned Call
				☐ Stopped By
				☐ Please Call
				☐ Wants to See You

Date	For	Name of Caller & Company	Time of Call	Delivery Time
Phone Number:	Email:			☐ Urgent
Message:				☐ Returned Call
				☐ Stopped By
				☐ Please Call
				☐ Wants to See You

Date	For	Name of Caller & Company	Time of Call	Delivery Time
Phone Number:	Email:			☐ Urgent
Message:				☐ Returned Call
				☐ Stopped By
				☐ Please Call
				☐ Wants to See You

Date	For	Name of Caller & Company	Time of Call	Delivery Time
Phone Number:	Email:			☐ Urgent
Message:				☐ Returned Call
				☐ Stopped By
				☐ Please Call
				☐ Wants to See You

Date	For	Name of Caller & Company	Time of Call	Delivery Time

Phone Number:	Email:	☐ Urgent
Message:		☐ Returned Call
		☐ Stopped By
		☐ Please Call
		☐ Wants to See You

Date	For	Name of Caller & Company	Time of Call	Delivery Time

Phone Number:	Email:	☐ Urgent
Message:		☐ Returned Call
		☐ Stopped By
		☐ Please Call
		☐ Wants to See You

Date	For	Name of Caller & Company	Time of Call	Delivery Time

Phone Number:	Email:	☐ Urgent
Message:		☐ Returned Call
		☐ Stopped By
		☐ Please Call
		☐ Wants to See You

Date	For	Name of Caller & Company	Time of Call	Delivery Time

Phone Number:	Email:	☐ Urgent
Message:		☐ Returned Call
		☐ Stopped By
		☐ Please Call
		☐ Wants to See You

Date	For	Name of Caller & Company	Time of Call	Delivery Time

Phone Number:	Email:	☐ Urgent
Message:		☐ Returned Call
		☐ Stopped By
		☐ Please Call
		☐ Wants to See You

Date	For	Name of Caller & Company	Time of Call	Delivery Time

Phone Number:	Email:	☐ Urgent
Message:		☐ Returned Call
		☐ Stopped By
		☐ Please Call
		☐ Wants to See You

Date	For	Name of Caller & Company	Time of Call	Delivery Time

Phone Number:	Email:	☐ Urgent
Message:		☐ Returned Call
		☐ Stopped By
		☐ Please Call
		☐ Wants to See You

Date	For	Name of Caller & Company	Time of Call	Delivery Time

Phone Number:	Email:	☐ Urgent
Message:		☐ Returned Call
		☐ Stopped By
		☐ Please Call
		☐ Wants to See You

Date	For	Name of Caller & Company	Time of Call	Delivery Time

Phone Number:	Email:	☐ Urgent
Message:		☐ Returned Call
		☐ Stopped By
		☐ Please Call
		☐ Wants to See You

Date	For	Name of Caller & Company	Time of Call	Delivery Time

Phone Number:	**Email:**	☐ Urgent
Message:		☐ Returned Call
		☐ Stopped By
		☐ Please Call
		☐ Wants to See You

Date	For	Name of Caller & Company	Time of Call	Delivery Time

Phone Number:	**Email:**	☐ Urgent
Message:		☐ Returned Call
		☐ Stopped By
		☐ Please Call
		☐ Wants to See You

Date	For	Name of Caller & Company	Time of Call	Delivery Time

Phone Number:	**Email:**	☐ Urgent
Message:		☐ Returned Call
		☐ Stopped By
		☐ Please Call
		☐ Wants to See You

Date	For	Name of Caller & Company	Time of Call	Delivery Time
Phone Number:		Email:		☐ Urgent
Message:				☐ Returned Call
				☐ Stopped By
				☐ Please Call
				☐ Wants to See You

Date	For	Name of Caller & Company	Time of Call	Delivery Time
Phone Number:		Email:		☐ Urgent
Message:				☐ Returned Call
				☐ Stopped By
				☐ Please Call
				☐ Wants to See You

Date	For	Name of Caller & Company	Time of Call	Delivery Time
Phone Number:		Email:		☐ Urgent
Message:				☐ Returned Call
				☐ Stopped By
				☐ Please Call
				☐ Wants to See You

Date	For	Name of Caller & Company	Time of Call	Delivery Time
Phone Number:	Email:			☐ Urgent
Message:				☐ Returned Call
				☐ Stopped By
				☐ Please Call
				☐ Wants to See You

Date	For	Name of Caller & Company	Time of Call	Delivery Time
Phone Number:	Email:			☐ Urgent
Message:				☐ Returned Call
				☐ Stopped By
				☐ Please Call
				☐ Wants to See You

Date	For	Name of Caller & Company	Time of Call	Delivery Time
Phone Number:	Email:			☐ Urgent
Message:				☐ Returned Call
				☐ Stopped By
				☐ Please Call
				☐ Wants to See You

Date	For	Name of Caller & Company	Time of Call	Delivery Time

Phone Number:	Email:	☐ Urgent
Message:		☐ Returned Call
		☐ Stopped By
		☐ Please Call
		☐ Wants to See You

Date	For	Name of Caller & Company	Time of Call	Delivery Time

Phone Number:	Email:	☐ Urgent
Message:		☐ Returned Call
		☐ Stopped By
		☐ Please Call
		☐ Wants to See You

Date	For	Name of Caller & Company	Time of Call	Delivery Time

Phone Number:	Email:	☐ Urgent
Message:		☐ Returned Call
		☐ Stopped By
		☐ Please Call
		☐ Wants to See You

Date	For	Name of Caller & Company	Time of Call	Delivery Time

Phone Number:	Email:	☐ Urgent
Message:		☐ Returned Call
		☐ Stopped By
		☐ Please Call
		☐ Wants to See You

Date	For	Name of Caller & Company	Time of Call	Delivery Time

Phone Number:	Email:	☐ Urgent
Message:		☐ Returned Call
		☐ Stopped By
		☐ Please Call
		☐ Wants to See You

Date	For	Name of Caller & Company	Time of Call	Delivery Time

Phone Number:	Email:	☐ Urgent
Message:		☐ Returned Call
		☐ Stopped By
		☐ Please Call
		☐ Wants to See You

Date	For	Name of Caller & Company	Time of Call	Delivery Time

Phone Number:	Email:	☐ Urgent
Message:		☐ Returned Call
		☐ Stopped By
		☐ Please Call
		☐ Wants to See You

Date	For	Name of Caller & Company	Time of Call	Delivery Time

Phone Number:	Email:	☐ Urgent
Message:		☐ Returned Call
		☐ Stopped By
		☐ Please Call
		☐ Wants to See You

Date	For	Name of Caller & Company	Time of Call	Delivery Time

Phone Number:	Email:	☐ Urgent
Message:		☐ Returned Call
		☐ Stopped By
		☐ Please Call
		☐ Wants to See You

Date	For	Name of Caller & Company	Time of Call	Delivery Time

Phone Number:	Email:	☐ Urgent
Message:		☐ Returned Call
		☐ Stopped By
		☐ Please Call
		☐ Wants to See You

Date	For	Name of Caller & Company	Time of Call	Delivery Time

Phone Number:	Email:	☐ Urgent
Message:		☐ Returned Call
		☐ Stopped By
		☐ Please Call
		☐ Wants to See You

Date	For	Name of Caller & Company	Time of Call	Delivery Time

Phone Number:	Email:	☐ Urgent
Message:		☐ Returned Call
		☐ Stopped By
		☐ Please Call
		☐ Wants to See You

Date	For	Name of Caller & Company	Time of Call	Delivery Time
Phone Number:		Email:		☐ Urgent
Message:				☐ Returned Call
				☐ Stopped By
				☐ Please Call
				☐ Wants to See You

Date	For	Name of Caller & Company	Time of Call	Delivery Time
Phone Number:		Email:		☐ Urgent
Message:				☐ Returned Call
				☐ Stopped By
				☐ Please Call
				☐ Wants to See You

Date	For	Name of Caller & Company	Time of Call	Delivery Time
Phone Number:		Email:		☐ Urgent
Message:				☐ Returned Call
				☐ Stopped By
				☐ Please Call
				☐ Wants to See You

Date	For	Name of Caller & Company	Time of Call	Delivery Time
Phone Number:	Email:			☐ Urgent
Message:				☐ Returned Call
				☐ Stopped By
				☐ Please Call
				☐ Wants to See You

Date	For	Name of Caller & Company	Time of Call	Delivery Time
Phone Number:	Email:			☐ Urgent
Message:				☐ Returned Call
				☐ Stopped By
				☐ Please Call
				☐ Wants to See You

Date	For	Name of Caller & Company	Time of Call	Delivery Time
Phone Number:	Email:			☐ Urgent
Message:				☐ Returned Call
				☐ Stopped By
				☐ Please Call
				☐ Wants to See You

Date	For	Name of Caller & Company	Time of Call	Delivery Time
Phone Number:		Email:		☐ Urgent
Message:				☐ Returned Call
				☐ Stopped By
				☐ Please Call
				☐ Wants to See You

Date	For	Name of Caller & Company	Time of Call	Delivery Time
Phone Number:		Email:		☐ Urgent
Message:				☐ Returned Call
				☐ Stopped By
				☐ Please Call
				☐ Wants to See You

Date	For	Name of Caller & Company	Time of Call	Delivery Time
Phone Number:		Email:		☐ Urgent
Message:				☐ Returned Call
				☐ Stopped By
				☐ Please Call
				☐ Wants to See You

Date	For	Name of Caller & Company	Time of Call	Delivery Time

Phone Number:	Email:	☐ Urgent
Message:		☐ Returned Call
		☐ Stopped By
		☐ Please Call
		☐ Wants to See You

Date	For	Name of Caller & Company	Time of Call	Delivery Time

Phone Number:	Email:	☐ Urgent
Message:		☐ Returned Call
		☐ Stopped By
		☐ Please Call
		☐ Wants to See You

Date	For	Name of Caller & Company	Time of Call	Delivery Time

Phone Number:	Email:	☐ Urgent
Message:		☐ Returned Call
		☐ Stopped By
		☐ Please Call
		☐ Wants to See You

Date	For	Name of Caller & Company	Time of Call	Delivery Time

Phone Number:	Email:	☐ Urgent
Message:		☐ Returned Call
		☐ Stopped By
		☐ Please Call
		☐ Wants to See You

Date	For	Name of Caller & Company	Time of Call	Delivery Time

Phone Number:	Email:	☐ Urgent
Message:		☐ Returned Call
		☐ Stopped By
		☐ Please Call
		☐ Wants to See You

Date	For	Name of Caller & Company	Time of Call	Delivery Time

Phone Number:	Email:	☐ Urgent
Message:		☐ Returned Call
		☐ Stopped By
		☐ Please Call
		☐ Wants to See You

Date	For	Name of Caller & Company	Time of Call	Delivery Time
Phone Number:		**Email:**		☐ Urgent
Message:				☐ Returned Call
				☐ Stopped By
				☐ Please Call
				☐ Wants to See You

Date	For	Name of Caller & Company	Time of Call	Delivery Time
Phone Number:		**Email:**		☐ Urgent
Message:				☐ Returned Call
				☐ Stopped By
				☐ Please Call
				☐ Wants to See You

Date	For	Name of Caller & Company	Time of Call	Delivery Time
Phone Number:		**Email:**		☐ Urgent
Message:				☐ Returned Call
				☐ Stopped By
				☐ Please Call
				☐ Wants to See You

Date	For	Name of Caller & Company	Time of Call	Delivery Time

Phone Number:	**Email:**	☐ Urgent
Message:		☐ Returned Call
		☐ Stopped By
		☐ Please Call
		☐ Wants to See You

Date	For	Name of Caller & Company	Time of Call	Delivery Time

Phone Number:	**Email:**	☐ Urgent
Message:		☐ Returned Call
		☐ Stopped By
		☐ Please Call
		☐ Wants to See You

Date	For	Name of Caller & Company	Time of Call	Delivery Time

Phone Number:	**Email:**	☐ Urgent
Message:		☐ Returned Call
		☐ Stopped By
		☐ Please Call
		☐ Wants to See You

Date	For	Name of Caller & Company	Time of Call	Delivery Time

Phone Number:	Email:	☐ Urgent
Message:		☐ Returned Call
		☐ Stopped By
		☐ Please Call
		☐ Wants to See You

Date	For	Name of Caller & Company	Time of Call	Delivery Time

Phone Number:	Email:	☐ Urgent
Message:		☐ Returned Call
		☐ Stopped By
		☐ Please Call
		☐ Wants to See You

Date	For	Name of Caller & Company	Time of Call	Delivery Time

Phone Number:	Email:	☐ Urgent
Message:		☐ Returned Call
		☐ Stopped By
		☐ Please Call
		☐ Wants to See You

Date	For	Name of Caller & Company	Time of Call	Delivery Time

Phone Number:	Email:	☐ Urgent
Message:		☐ Returned Call
		☐ Stopped By
		☐ Please Call
		☐ Wants to See You

Date	For	Name of Caller & Company	Time of Call	Delivery Time

Phone Number:	Email:	☐ Urgent
Message:		☐ Returned Call
		☐ Stopped By
		☐ Please Call
		☐ Wants to See You

Date	For	Name of Caller & Company	Time of Call	Delivery Time

Phone Number:	Email:	☐ Urgent
Message:		☐ Returned Call
		☐ Stopped By
		☐ Please Call
		☐ Wants to See You

Date	For	Name of Caller & Company	Time of Call	Delivery Time

Phone Number:	Email:	☐ Urgent
Message:		☐ Returned Call
		☐ Stopped By
		☐ Please Call
		☐ Wants to See You

Date	For	Name of Caller & Company	Time of Call	Delivery Time

Phone Number:	Email:	☐ Urgent
Message:		☐ Returned Call
		☐ Stopped By
		☐ Please Call
		☐ Wants to See You

Date	For	Name of Caller & Company	Time of Call	Delivery Time

Phone Number:	Email:	☐ Urgent
Message:		☐ Returned Call
		☐ Stopped By
		☐ Please Call
		☐ Wants to See You

Date	For	Name of Caller & Company	Time of Call	Delivery Time

Phone Number:	Email:	☐ Urgent
Message:		☐ Returned Call
		☐ Stopped By
		☐ Please Call
		☐ Wants to See You

Date	For	Name of Caller & Company	Time of Call	Delivery Time

Phone Number:	Email:	☐ Urgent
Message:		☐ Returned Call
		☐ Stopped By
		☐ Please Call
		☐ Wants to See You

Date	For	Name of Caller & Company	Time of Call	Delivery Time

Phone Number:	Email:	☐ Urgent
Message:		☐ Returned Call
		☐ Stopped By
		☐ Please Call
		☐ Wants to See You

Date	For	Name of Caller & Company	Time of Call	Delivery Time

Phone Number:	Email:	☐ Urgent
Message:		☐ Returned Call
		☐ Stopped By
		☐ Please Call
		☐ Wants to See You

Date	For	Name of Caller & Company	Time of Call	Delivery Time

Phone Number:	Email:	☐ Urgent
Message:		☐ Returned Call
		☐ Stopped By
		☐ Please Call
		☐ Wants to See You

Date	For	Name of Caller & Company	Time of Call	Delivery Time

Phone Number:	Email:	☐ Urgent
Message:		☐ Returned Call
		☐ Stopped By
		☐ Please Call
		☐ Wants to See You

Date	For	Name of Caller & Company	Time of Call	Delivery Time
Phone Number:	**Email:**			☐ Urgent
Message:				☐ Returned Call
				☐ Stopped By
				☐ Please Call
				☐ Wants to See You

Date	For	Name of Caller & Company	Time of Call	Delivery Time
Phone Number:	**Email:**			☐ Urgent
Message:				☐ Returned Call
				☐ Stopped By
				☐ Please Call
				☐ Wants to See You

Date	For	Name of Caller & Company	Time of Call	Delivery Time
Phone Number:	**Email:**			☐ Urgent
Message:				☐ Returned Call
				☐ Stopped By
				☐ Please Call
				☐ Wants to See You

Date	For	Name of Caller & Company	Time of Call	Delivery Time

Phone Number:	Email:	☐ Urgent
Message:		☐ Returned Call
		☐ Stopped By
		☐ Please Call
		☐ Wants to See You

Date	For	Name of Caller & Company	Time of Call	Delivery Time

Phone Number:	Email:	☐ Urgent
Message:		☐ Returned Call
		☐ Stopped By
		☐ Please Call
		☐ Wants to See You

Date	For	Name of Caller & Company	Time of Call	Delivery Time

Phone Number:	Email:	☐ Urgent
Message:		☐ Returned Call
		☐ Stopped By
		☐ Please Call
		☐ Wants to See You

Date	For	Name of Caller & Company	Time of Call	Delivery Time

Phone Number:	Email:	☐ Urgent
Message:		☐ Returned Call
		☐ Stopped By
		☐ Please Call
		☐ Wants to See You

Date	For	Name of Caller & Company	Time of Call	Delivery Time

Phone Number:	Email:	☐ Urgent
Message:		☐ Returned Call
		☐ Stopped By
		☐ Please Call
		☐ Wants to See You

Date	For	Name of Caller & Company	Time of Call	Delivery Time

Phone Number:	Email:	☐ Urgent
Message:		☐ Returned Call
		☐ Stopped By
		☐ Please Call
		☐ Wants to See You

Date	For	Name of Caller & Company	Time of Call	Delivery Time

Phone Number:	Email:	☐ Urgent
Message:		☐ Returned Call
		☐ Stopped By
		☐ Please Call
		☐ Wants to See You

Date	For	Name of Caller & Company	Time of Call	Delivery Time

Phone Number:	Email:	☐ Urgent
Message:		☐ Returned Call
		☐ Stopped By
		☐ Please Call
		☐ Wants to See You

Date	For	Name of Caller & Company	Time of Call	Delivery Time

Phone Number:	Email:	☐ Urgent
Message:		☐ Returned Call
		☐ Stopped By
		☐ Please Call
		☐ Wants to See You

Date	For	Name of Caller & Company	Time of Call	Delivery Time

Phone Number:	Email:	☐ Urgent
Message:		☐ Returned Call
		☐ Stopped By
		☐ Please Call
		☐ Wants to See You

Date	For	Name of Caller & Company	Time of Call	Delivery Time

Phone Number:	Email:	☐ Urgent
Message:		☐ Returned Call
		☐ Stopped By
		☐ Please Call
		☐ Wants to See You

Date	For	Name of Caller & Company	Time of Call	Delivery Time

Phone Number:	Email:	☐ Urgent
Message:		☐ Returned Call
		☐ Stopped By
		☐ Please Call
		☐ Wants to See You

Date	For	Name of Caller & Company	Time of Call	Delivery Time
Phone Number:		Email:		☐ Urgent
Message:				☐ Returned Call
				☐ Stopped By
				☐ Please Call
				☐ Wants to See You

Date	For	Name of Caller & Company	Time of Call	Delivery Time
Phone Number:		Email:		☐ Urgent
Message:				☐ Returned Call
				☐ Stopped By
				☐ Please Call
				☐ Wants to See You

Date	For	Name of Caller & Company	Time of Call	Delivery Time
Phone Number:		Email:		☐ Urgent
Message:				☐ Returned Call
				☐ Stopped By
				☐ Please Call
				☐ Wants to See You

Date	For	Name of Caller & Company	Time of Call	Delivery Time
Phone Number:		**Email:**		☐ Urgent
Message:				☐ Returned Call
				☐ Stopped By
				☐ Please Call
				☐ Wants to See You

Date	For	Name of Caller & Company	Time of Call	Delivery Time
Phone Number:		**Email:**		☐ Urgent
Message:				☐ Returned Call
				☐ Stopped By
				☐ Please Call
				☐ Wants to See You

Date	For	Name of Caller & Company	Time of Call	Delivery Time
Phone Number:		**Email:**		☐ Urgent
Message:				☐ Returned Call
				☐ Stopped By
				☐ Please Call
				☐ Wants to See You

Date	For	Name of Caller & Company	Time of Call	Delivery Time

Phone Number:	Email:	☐ Urgent
Message:		☐ Returned Call
		☐ Stopped By
		☐ Please Call
		☐ Wants to See You

Date	For	Name of Caller & Company	Time of Call	Delivery Time

Phone Number:	Email:	☐ Urgent
Message:		☐ Returned Call
		☐ Stopped By
		☐ Please Call
		☐ Wants to See You

Date	For	Name of Caller & Company	Time of Call	Delivery Time

Phone Number:	Email:	☐ Urgent
Message:		☐ Returned Call
		☐ Stopped By
		☐ Please Call
		☐ Wants to See You

Date	For	Name of Caller & Company	Time of Call	Delivery Time

Phone Number:	Email:	☐ Urgent
Message:		☐ Returned Call
		☐ Stopped By
		☐ Please Call
		☐ Wants to See You

Date	For	Name of Caller & Company	Time of Call	Delivery Time

Phone Number:	Email:	☐ Urgent
Message:		☐ Returned Call
		☐ Stopped By
		☐ Please Call
		☐ Wants to See You

Date	For	Name of Caller & Company	Time of Call	Delivery Time

Phone Number:	Email:	☐ Urgent
Message:		☐ Returned Call
		☐ Stopped By
		☐ Please Call
		☐ Wants to See You

Date	For	Name of Caller & Company	Time of Call	Delivery Time

Phone Number:	Email:	☐ Urgent
Message:		☐ Returned Call
		☐ Stopped By
		☐ Please Call
		☐ Wants to See You

Date	For	Name of Caller & Company	Time of Call	Delivery Time

Phone Number:	Email:	☐ Urgent
Message:		☐ Returned Call
		☐ Stopped By
		☐ Please Call
		☐ Wants to See You

Date	For	Name of Caller & Company	Time of Call	Delivery Time

Phone Number:	Email:	☐ Urgent
Message:		☐ Returned Call
		☐ Stopped By
		☐ Please Call
		☐ Wants to See You

Date	For	Name of Caller & Company	Time of Call	Delivery Time

Phone Number:	Email:	☐ Urgent
Message:		☐ Returned Call
		☐ Stopped By
		☐ Please Call
		☐ Wants to See You

Date	For	Name of Caller & Company	Time of Call	Delivery Time

Phone Number:	Email:	☐ Urgent
Message:		☐ Returned Call
		☐ Stopped By
		☐ Please Call
		☐ Wants to See You

Date	For	Name of Caller & Company	Time of Call	Delivery Time

Phone Number:	Email:	☐ Urgent
Message:		☐ Returned Call
		☐ Stopped By
		☐ Please Call
		☐ Wants to See You

Date	For	Name of Caller & Company	Time of Call	Delivery Time

Phone Number:	Email:	☐ Urgent
Message:		☐ Returned Call
		☐ Stopped By
		☐ Please Call
		☐ Wants to See You

Date	For	Name of Caller & Company	Time of Call	Delivery Time

Phone Number:	Email:	☐ Urgent
Message:		☐ Returned Call
		☐ Stopped By
		☐ Please Call
		☐ Wants to See You

Date	For	Name of Caller & Company	Time of Call	Delivery Time

Phone Number:	Email:	☐ Urgent
Message:		☐ Returned Call
		☐ Stopped By
		☐ Please Call
		☐ Wants to See You

Date	For	Name of Caller & Company	Time of Call	Delivery Time

Phone Number:	Email:	☐ Urgent
Message:		☐ Returned Call
		☐ Stopped By
		☐ Please Call
		☐ Wants to See You

Date	For	Name of Caller & Company	Time of Call	Delivery Time

Phone Number:	Email:	☐ Urgent
Message:		☐ Returned Call
		☐ Stopped By
		☐ Please Call
		☐ Wants to See You

Date	For	Name of Caller & Company	Time of Call	Delivery Time

Phone Number:	Email:	☐ Urgent
Message:		☐ Returned Call
		☐ Stopped By
		☐ Please Call
		☐ Wants to See You

Date	For	Name of Caller & Company	Time of Call	Delivery Time

Phone Number:	Email:	☐ Urgent
Message:		☐ Returned Call
		☐ Stopped By
		☐ Please Call
		☐ Wants to See You

Date	For	Name of Caller & Company	Time of Call	Delivery Time

Phone Number:	Email:	☐ Urgent
Message:		☐ Returned Call
		☐ Stopped By
		☐ Please Call
		☐ Wants to See You

Date	For	Name of Caller & Company	Time of Call	Delivery Time

Phone Number:	Email:	☐ Urgent
Message:		☐ Returned Call
		☐ Stopped By
		☐ Please Call
		☐ Wants to See You

Date	For	Name of Caller & Company	Time of Call	Delivery Time

Phone Number:	Email:	☐ Urgent
Message:		☐ Returned Call
		☐ Stopped By
		☐ Please Call
		☐ Wants to See You

Date	For	Name of Caller & Company	Time of Call	Delivery Time

Phone Number:	Email:	☐ Urgent
Message:		☐ Returned Call
		☐ Stopped By
		☐ Please Call
		☐ Wants to See You

Date	For	Name of Caller & Company	Time of Call	Delivery Time

Phone Number:	Email:	☐ Urgent
Message:		☐ Returned Call
		☐ Stopped By
		☐ Please Call
		☐ Wants to See You

Date	For	Name of Caller & Company	Time of Call	Delivery Time

Phone Number:	Email:	☐ Urgent
Message:		☐ Returned Call
		☐ Stopped By
		☐ Please Call
		☐ Wants to See You

Date	For	Name of Caller & Company	Time of Call	Delivery Time

Phone Number:	Email:	☐ Urgent
Message:		☐ Returned Call
		☐ Stopped By
		☐ Please Call
		☐ Wants to See You

Date	For	Name of Caller & Company	Time of Call	Delivery Time

Phone Number:	Email:	☐ Urgent
Message:		☐ Returned Call
		☐ Stopped By
		☐ Please Call
		☐ Wants to See You

Date	For	Name of Caller & Company	Time of Call	Delivery Time

Phone Number:	Email:	☐ Urgent
Message:		☐ Returned Call
		☐ Stopped By
		☐ Please Call
		☐ Wants to See You

Date	For	Name of Caller & Company	Time of Call	Delivery Time

Phone Number:	Email:	☐ Urgent
Message:		☐ Returned Call
		☐ Stopped By
		☐ Please Call
		☐ Wants to See You

Date	For	Name of Caller & Company	Time of Call	Delivery Time

Phone Number:	Email:	☐ Urgent
Message:		☐ Returned Call
		☐ Stopped By
		☐ Please Call
		☐ Wants to See You

Date	For	Name of Caller & Company	Time of Call	Delivery Time
Phone Number:		Email:		☐ Urgent
Message:				☐ Returned Call
				☐ Stopped By
				☐ Please Call
				☐ Wants to See You

Date	For	Name of Caller & Company	Time of Call	Delivery Time
Phone Number:		Email:		☐ Urgent
Message:				☐ Returned Call
				☐ Stopped By
				☐ Please Call
				☐ Wants to See You

Date	For	Name of Caller & Company	Time of Call	Delivery Time
Phone Number:		Email:		☐ Urgent
Message:				☐ Returned Call
				☐ Stopped By
				☐ Please Call
				☐ Wants to See You

Date	For	Name of Caller & Company	Time of Call	Delivery Time

Phone Number:	Email:	☐ Urgent
Message:		☐ Returned Call
		☐ Stopped By
		☐ Please Call
		☐ Wants to See You

Date	For	Name of Caller & Company	Time of Call	Delivery Time

Phone Number:	Email:	☐ Urgent
Message:		☐ Returned Call
		☐ Stopped By
		☐ Please Call
		☐ Wants to See You

Date	For	Name of Caller & Company	Time of Call	Delivery Time

Phone Number:	Email:	☐ Urgent
Message:		☐ Returned Call
		☐ Stopped By
		☐ Please Call
		☐ Wants to See You

Date	For	Name of Caller & Company	Time of Call	Delivery Time

Phone Number:	Email:	☐ Urgent
Message:		☐ Returned Call
		☐ Stopped By
		☐ Please Call
		☐ Wants to See You

Date	For	Name of Caller & Company	Time of Call	Delivery Time

Phone Number:	Email:	☐ Urgent
Message:		☐ Returned Call
		☐ Stopped By
		☐ Please Call
		☐ Wants to See You

Date	For	Name of Caller & Company	Time of Call	Delivery Time

Phone Number:	Email:	☐ Urgent
Message:		☐ Returned Call
		☐ Stopped By
		☐ Please Call
		☐ Wants to See You

Date	For	Name of Caller & Company	Time of Call	Delivery Time

Phone Number:	Email:	☐ Urgent
Message:		☐ Returned Call
		☐ Stopped By
		☐ Please Call
		☐ Wants to See You

Date	For	Name of Caller & Company	Time of Call	Delivery Time

Phone Number:	Email:	☐ Urgent
Message:		☐ Returned Call
		☐ Stopped By
		☐ Please Call
		☐ Wants to See You

Date	For	Name of Caller & Company	Time of Call	Delivery Time

Phone Number:	Email:	☐ Urgent
Message:		☐ Returned Call
		☐ Stopped By
		☐ Please Call
		☐ Wants to See You

Date	For	Name of Caller & Company	Time of Call	Delivery Time

Phone Number:	Email:	☐ Urgent
Message:		☐ Returned Call
		☐ Stopped By
		☐ Please Call
		☐ Wants to See You

Date	For	Name of Caller & Company	Time of Call	Delivery Time

Phone Number:	Email:	☐ Urgent
Message:		☐ Returned Call
		☐ Stopped By
		☐ Please Call
		☐ Wants to See You

Date	For	Name of Caller & Company	Time of Call	Delivery Time

Phone Number:	Email:	☐ Urgent
Message:		☐ Returned Call
		☐ Stopped By
		☐ Please Call
		☐ Wants to See You

Date	For	Name of Caller & Company	Time of Call	Delivery Time

Phone Number:	Email:	☐ Urgent
Message:		☐ Returned Call
		☐ Stopped By
		☐ Please Call
		☐ Wants to See You

Date	For	Name of Caller & Company	Time of Call	Delivery Time

Phone Number:	Email:	☐ Urgent
Message:		☐ Returned Call
		☐ Stopped By
		☐ Please Call
		☐ Wants to See You

Date	For	Name of Caller & Company	Time of Call	Delivery Time

Phone Number:	Email:	☐ Urgent
Message:		☐ Returned Call
		☐ Stopped By
		☐ Please Call
		☐ Wants to See You

Date	For	Name of Caller & Company	Time of Call	Delivery Time

Phone Number:	Email:	☐ Urgent
Message:		☐ Returned Call
		☐ Stopped By
		☐ Please Call
		☐ Wants to See You

Date	For	Name of Caller & Company	Time of Call	Delivery Time

Phone Number:	Email:	☐ Urgent
Message:		☐ Returned Call
		☐ Stopped By
		☐ Please Call
		☐ Wants to See You

Date	For	Name of Caller & Company	Time of Call	Delivery Time

Phone Number:	Email:	☐ Urgent
Message:		☐ Returned Call
		☐ Stopped By
		☐ Please Call
		☐ Wants to See You

Date	For	Name of Caller & Company	Time of Call	Delivery Time
Phone Number:		Email:		☐ Urgent
Message:				☐ Returned Call
				☐ Stopped By
				☐ Please Call
				☐ Wants to See You

Date	For	Name of Caller & Company	Time of Call	Delivery Time
Phone Number:		Email:		☐ Urgent
Message:				☐ Returned Call
				☐ Stopped By
				☐ Please Call
				☐ Wants to See You

Date	For	Name of Caller & Company	Time of Call	Delivery Time
Phone Number:		Email:		☐ Urgent
Message:				☐ Returned Call
				☐ Stopped By
				☐ Please Call
				☐ Wants to See You

Date	For	Name of Caller & Company	Time of Call	Delivery Time

Phone Number:		Email:		☐ Urgent
Message:				☐ Returned Call
				☐ Stopped By
				☐ Please Call
				☐ Wants to See You

Date	For	Name of Caller & Company	Time of Call	Delivery Time

Phone Number:		Email:		☐ Urgent
Message:				☐ Returned Call
				☐ Stopped By
				☐ Please Call
				☐ Wants to See You

Date	For	Name of Caller & Company	Time of Call	Delivery Time

Phone Number:		Email:		☐ Urgent
Message:				☐ Returned Call
				☐ Stopped By
				☐ Please Call
				☐ Wants to See You

Date	For	Name of Caller & Company	Time of Call	Delivery Time

Phone Number:	Email:	☐ Urgent
Message:		☐ Returned Call
		☐ Stopped By
		☐ Please Call
		☐ Wants to See You

Date	For	Name of Caller & Company	Time of Call	Delivery Time

Phone Number:	Email:	☐ Urgent
Message:		☐ Returned Call
		☐ Stopped By
		☐ Please Call
		☐ Wants to See You

Date	For	Name of Caller & Company	Time of Call	Delivery Time

Phone Number:	Email:	☐ Urgent
Message:		☐ Returned Call
		☐ Stopped By
		☐ Please Call
		☐ Wants to See You

Date	For	Name of Caller & Company	Time of Call	Delivery Time

Phone Number:	Email:	☐ Urgent
Message:		☐ Returned Call
		☐ Stopped By
		☐ Please Call
		☐ Wants to See You

Date	For	Name of Caller & Company	Time of Call	Delivery Time

Phone Number:	Email:	☐ Urgent
Message:		☐ Returned Call
		☐ Stopped By
		☐ Please Call
		☐ Wants to See You

Date	For	Name of Caller & Company	Time of Call	Delivery Time

Phone Number:	Email:	☐ Urgent
Message:		☐ Returned Call
		☐ Stopped By
		☐ Please Call
		☐ Wants to See You

Date	For	Name of Caller & Company	Time of Call	Delivery Time

Phone Number:	Email:	☐ Urgent
Message:		☐ Returned Call
		☐ Stopped By
		☐ Please Call
		☐ Wants to See You

Date	For	Name of Caller & Company	Time of Call	Delivery Time

Phone Number:	Email:	☐ Urgent
Message:		☐ Returned Call
		☐ Stopped By
		☐ Please Call
		☐ Wants to See You

Date	For	Name of Caller & Company	Time of Call	Delivery Time

Phone Number:	Email:	☐ Urgent
Message:		☐ Returned Call
		☐ Stopped By
		☐ Please Call
		☐ Wants to See You

Date	For	Name of Caller & Company	Time of Call	Delivery Time

Phone Number:	Email:	☐ Urgent
Message:		☐ Returned Call
		☐ Stopped By
		☐ Please Call
		☐ Wants to See You

Date	For	Name of Caller & Company	Time of Call	Delivery Time

Phone Number:	Email:	☐ Urgent
Message:		☐ Returned Call
		☐ Stopped By
		☐ Please Call
		☐ Wants to See You

Date	For	Name of Caller & Company	Time of Call	Delivery Time

Phone Number:	Email:	☐ Urgent
Message:		☐ Returned Call
		☐ Stopped By
		☐ Please Call
		☐ Wants to See You

Date	For	Name of Caller & Company	Time of Call	Delivery Time

Phone Number:	Email:	☐ Urgent
Message:		☐ Returned Call
		☐ Stopped By
		☐ Please Call
		☐ Wants to See You

Date	For	Name of Caller & Company	Time of Call	Delivery Time

Phone Number:	Email:	☐ Urgent
Message:		☐ Returned Call
		☐ Stopped By
		☐ Please Call
		☐ Wants to See You

Date	For	Name of Caller & Company	Time of Call	Delivery Time

Phone Number:	Email:	☐ Urgent
Message:		☐ Returned Call
		☐ Stopped By
		☐ Please Call
		☐ Wants to See You

Date	For	Name of Caller & Company	Time of Call	Delivery Time

Phone Number:	Email:	☐ Urgent
Message:		☐ Returned Call
		☐ Stopped By
		☐ Please Call
		☐ Wants to See You

Date	For	Name of Caller & Company	Time of Call	Delivery Time

Phone Number:	Email:	☐ Urgent
Message:		☐ Returned Call
		☐ Stopped By
		☐ Please Call
		☐ Wants to See You

Date	For	Name of Caller & Company	Time of Call	Delivery Time

Phone Number:	Email:	☐ Urgent
Message:		☐ Returned Call
		☐ Stopped By
		☐ Please Call
		☐ Wants to See You

Date	For	Name of Caller & Company	Time of Call	Delivery Time

Phone Number:	Email:	☐ Urgent
Message:		☐ Returned Call
		☐ Stopped By
		☐ Please Call
		☐ Wants to See You

Date	For	Name of Caller & Company	Time of Call	Delivery Time

Phone Number:	Email:	☐ Urgent
Message:		☐ Returned Call
		☐ Stopped By
		☐ Please Call
		☐ Wants to See You

Date	For	Name of Caller & Company	Time of Call	Delivery Time

Phone Number:	Email:	☐ Urgent
Message:		☐ Returned Call
		☐ Stopped By
		☐ Please Call
		☐ Wants to See You

Date	For	Name of Caller & Company	Time of Call	Delivery Time

Phone Number:	Email:	☐ Urgent
Message:		☐ Returned Call
		☐ Stopped By
		☐ Please Call
		☐ Wants to See You

Date	For	Name of Caller & Company	Time of Call	Delivery Time

Phone Number:	Email:	☐ Urgent
Message:		☐ Returned Call
		☐ Stopped By
		☐ Please Call
		☐ Wants to See You

Date	For	Name of Caller & Company	Time of Call	Delivery Time

Phone Number:	Email:	☐ Urgent
Message:		☐ Returned Call
		☐ Stopped By
		☐ Please Call
		☐ Wants to See You

Date	For	Name of Caller & Company	Time of Call	Delivery Time

Phone Number:		Email:		☐ Urgent
Message:				☐ Returned Call
				☐ Stopped By
				☐ Please Call
				☐ Wants to See You

Date	For	Name of Caller & Company	Time of Call	Delivery Time

Phone Number:		Email:		☐ Urgent
Message:				☐ Returned Call
				☐ Stopped By
				☐ Please Call
				☐ Wants to See You

Date	For	Name of Caller & Company	Time of Call	Delivery Time

Phone Number:		Email:		☐ Urgent
Message:				☐ Returned Call
				☐ Stopped By
				☐ Please Call
				☐ Wants to See You

Date	For	Name of Caller & Company	Time of Call	Delivery Time

Phone Number:	Email:	☐ Urgent
Message:		☐ Returned Call
		☐ Stopped By
		☐ Please Call
		☐ Wants to See You

Date	For	Name of Caller & Company	Time of Call	Delivery Time

Phone Number:	Email:	☐ Urgent
Message:		☐ Returned Call
		☐ Stopped By
		☐ Please Call
		☐ Wants to See You

Date	For	Name of Caller & Company	Time of Call	Delivery Time

Phone Number:	Email:	☐ Urgent
Message:		☐ Returned Call
		☐ Stopped By
		☐ Please Call
		☐ Wants to See You

Date	For	Name of Caller & Company	Time of Call	Delivery Time

Phone Number:	Email:	☐ Urgent
Message:		☐ Returned Call
		☐ Stopped By
		☐ Please Call
		☐ Wants to See You

Date	For	Name of Caller & Company	Time of Call	Delivery Time

Phone Number:	Email:	☐ Urgent
Message:		☐ Returned Call
		☐ Stopped By
		☐ Please Call
		☐ Wants to See You

Date	For	Name of Caller & Company	Time of Call	Delivery Time

Phone Number:	Email:	☐ Urgent
Message:		☐ Returned Call
		☐ Stopped By
		☐ Please Call
		☐ Wants to See You

Date	For	Name of Caller & Company	Time of Call	Delivery Time
Phone Number:		Email:		☐ Urgent
Message:				☐ Returned Call
				☐ Stopped By
				☐ Please Call
				☐ Wants to See You

Date	For	Name of Caller & Company	Time of Call	Delivery Time
Phone Number:		Email:		☐ Urgent
Message:				☐ Returned Call
				☐ Stopped By
				☐ Please Call
				☐ Wants to See You

Date	For	Name of Caller & Company	Time of Call	Delivery Time
Phone Number:		Email:		☐ Urgent
Message:				☐ Returned Call
				☐ Stopped By
				☐ Please Call
				☐ Wants to See You

Date	For	Name of Caller & Company	Time of Call	Delivery Time

Phone Number:	Email:	☐ Urgent
Message:		☐ Returned Call
		☐ Stopped By
		☐ Please Call
		☐ Wants to See You

Date	For	Name of Caller & Company	Time of Call	Delivery Time

Phone Number:	Email:	☐ Urgent
Message:		☐ Returned Call
		☐ Stopped By
		☐ Please Call
		☐ Wants to See You

Date	For	Name of Caller & Company	Time of Call	Delivery Time

Phone Number:	Email:	☐ Urgent
Message:		☐ Returned Call
		☐ Stopped By
		☐ Please Call
		☐ Wants to See You

Date	For	Name of Caller & Company	Time of Call	Delivery Time

Phone Number:	Email:	☐ Urgent
Message:		☐ Returned Call
		☐ Stopped By
		☐ Please Call
		☐ Wants to See You

Date	For	Name of Caller & Company	Time of Call	Delivery Time

Phone Number:	Email:	☐ Urgent
Message:		☐ Returned Call
		☐ Stopped By
		☐ Please Call
		☐ Wants to See You

Date	For	Name of Caller & Company	Time of Call	Delivery Time

Phone Number:	Email:	☐ Urgent
Message:		☐ Returned Call
		☐ Stopped By
		☐ Please Call
		☐ Wants to See You

Date	For	Name of Caller & Company	Time of Call	Delivery Time
Phone Number:	Email:			☐ Urgent
Message:				☐ Returned Call
				☐ Stopped By
				☐ Please Call
				☐ Wants to See You

Date	For	Name of Caller & Company	Time of Call	Delivery Time
Phone Number:	Email:			☐ Urgent
Message:				☐ Returned Call
				☐ Stopped By
				☐ Please Call
				☐ Wants to See You

Date	For	Name of Caller & Company	Time of Call	Delivery Time
Phone Number:	Email:			☐ Urgent
Message:				☐ Returned Call
				☐ Stopped By
				☐ Please Call
				☐ Wants to See You

Date	For	Name of Caller & Company	Time of Call	Delivery Time
Phone Number:		Email:		☐ Urgent
Message:				☐ Returned Call
				☐ Stopped By
				☐ Please Call
				☐ Wants to See You

Date	For	Name of Caller & Company	Time of Call	Delivery Time
Phone Number:		Email:		☐ Urgent
Message:				☐ Returned Call
				☐ Stopped By
				☐ Please Call
				☐ Wants to See You

Date	For	Name of Caller & Company	Time of Call	Delivery Time
Phone Number:		Email:		☐ Urgent
Message:				☐ Returned Call
				☐ Stopped By
				☐ Please Call
				☐ Wants to See You

Date	For	Name of Caller & Company	Time of Call	Delivery Time
Phone Number:		Email:		☐ Urgent
Message:				☐ Returned Call
				☐ Stopped By
				☐ Please Call
				☐ Wants to See You

Date	For	Name of Caller & Company	Time of Call	Delivery Time
Phone Number:		Email:		☐ Urgent
Message:				☐ Returned Call
				☐ Stopped By
				☐ Please Call
				☐ Wants to See You

Date	For	Name of Caller & Company	Time of Call	Delivery Time
Phone Number:		Email:		☐ Urgent
Message:				☐ Returned Call
				☐ Stopped By
				☐ Please Call
				☐ Wants to See You

Date	For	Name of Caller & Company	Time of Call	Delivery Time

Phone Number:	Email:	☐ Urgent
Message:		☐ Returned Call
		☐ Stopped By
		☐ Please Call
		☐ Wants to See You

Date	For	Name of Caller & Company	Time of Call	Delivery Time

Phone Number:	Email:	☐ Urgent
Message:		☐ Returned Call
		☐ Stopped By
		☐ Please Call
		☐ Wants to See You

Date	For	Name of Caller & Company	Time of Call	Delivery Time

Phone Number:	Email:	☐ Urgent
Message:		☐ Returned Call
		☐ Stopped By
		☐ Please Call
		☐ Wants to See You

Date	For	Name of Caller & Company	Time of Call	Delivery Time

Phone Number:	Email:	☐ Urgent
Message:		☐ Returned Call
		☐ Stopped By
		☐ Please Call
		☐ Wants to See You

Date	For	Name of Caller & Company	Time of Call	Delivery Time

Phone Number:	Email:	☐ Urgent
Message:		☐ Returned Call
		☐ Stopped By
		☐ Please Call
		☐ Wants to See You

Date	For	Name of Caller & Company	Time of Call	Delivery Time

Phone Number:	Email:	☐ Urgent
Message:		☐ Returned Call
		☐ Stopped By
		☐ Please Call
		☐ Wants to See You

Date	For	Name of Caller & Company	Time of Call	Delivery Time

Phone Number:	Email:	☐ Urgent
Message:		☐ Returned Call
		☐ Stopped By
		☐ Please Call
		☐ Wants to See You

Date	For	Name of Caller & Company	Time of Call	Delivery Time

Phone Number:	Email:	☐ Urgent
Message:		☐ Returned Call
		☐ Stopped By
		☐ Please Call
		☐ Wants to See You

Date	For	Name of Caller & Company	Time of Call	Delivery Time

Phone Number:	Email:	☐ Urgent
Message:		☐ Returned Call
		☐ Stopped By
		☐ Please Call
		☐ Wants to See You

Date	For	Name of Caller & Company	Time of Call	Delivery Time

Phone Number:	Email:	☐ Urgent
Message:		☐ Returned Call
		☐ Stopped By
		☐ Please Call
		☐ Wants to See You

Date	For	Name of Caller & Company	Time of Call	Delivery Time

Phone Number:	Email:	☐ Urgent
Message:		☐ Returned Call
		☐ Stopped By
		☐ Please Call
		☐ Wants to See You

Date	For	Name of Caller & Company	Time of Call	Delivery Time

Phone Number:	Email:	☐ Urgent
Message:		☐ Returned Call
		☐ Stopped By
		☐ Please Call
		☐ Wants to See You

Date	For	Name of Caller & Company	Time of Call	Delivery Time

Phone Number:	Email:	☐ Urgent
Message:		☐ Returned Call
		☐ Stopped By
		☐ Please Call
		☐ Wants to See You

Date	For	Name of Caller & Company	Time of Call	Delivery Time

Phone Number:	Email:	☐ Urgent
Message:		☐ Returned Call
		☐ Stopped By
		☐ Please Call
		☐ Wants to See You

Date	For	Name of Caller & Company	Time of Call	Delivery Time

Phone Number:	Email:	☐ Urgent
Message:		☐ Returned Call
		☐ Stopped By
		☐ Please Call
		☐ Wants to See You

www.ingramcontent.com/pod-product-compliance
Lightning Source LLC
Chambersburg PA
CBHW081156180526
45170CB00006B/2100